# Nude as Retrospect

Alex Marlow

Out-Spoken Press
London

Published by Out-Spoken Press,
PO Box 78744,
London, N11 9FG

A CIP record for this title is available from the British Library.

First edition published 2023
ISBN: 978-1-7392652-3-6

Typeset in Adobe Caslon
Design by Patricia Ferguson
Printed and bound by Print Resources

Out-Spoken Press is supported using public funding by the National
Lottery through Arts Council England.

Supported using public funding by

**ARTS COUNCIL
ENGLAND**

# Contents

aloe   1

Dogwater   2

Fag's Dream   3

     I   3

     II   4

     III   5

     IV   6

     V   7

     VI   8

     VII   9

On the A56 to Accrington   10

Maybe I'll Be A Waitress   11

Hiber   12

wow   13

the pearls   14

Nude as Retrospect   15

fog head   16

jean jacket   17

whistle bitch   18

There Are No Bombs After 3pm   19

On Becoming A Mannequin   20

the unfinished business   21

Acknowledgements   23

## aloe

when the hallway light goes out
    then we can talk.
it's impossible to keep a family
    clean      no one can —
not the plants loosening their walls
    so a building becomes a home.
problems skirt themselves
    hanging teacloths
to dry out the consequence.
    this house commits amnesia
how else could it stay upright?
    son-child    haven't you
also made wicked decisions?
    remembered the animal of you
who'd rip out
    the precious aloe
shake the impermanence off
    its arid roots —

# Dogwater

Aren't nights       across the whole world
        low this year?


     — so drawn out
practice hasn't yet fastened itself to the ground
      an open sail cursing through.


At home the ceiling crawls all day.
      Stretch to night       to a controller
indenting hands with routine addictions.


Disappearance has to stop feeling this good.


You keep looking —
           God
    for fruits
       stuffed with white.


Girls pull the tails of spaniels out of brooks
      bake them into pill packets


      there's an understanding this time:


help did what it knew best       & ran.

# Fag's Dream

## I
*after Wilfred Owen*

What's done in dark can be done in light.
Your ability to disappear in metaphor
through walls at the sight & circus of law.
Flooded corridors, the pier hidden
concrete & cock, we're still glinting there.
Sanitised life to make a synonym for dead
where a phantom can fuck his history away.
In my bedroom eye, husbands turn supplicant.
I too drip in silver — you're no ghost or shadow.
Just a gem cut anew or bright lamp of dusk
fading into night, its men, & the devouring dawn.
Like you, I fall hard & fast for love —
one of my many deaths. Even now
it's happening again.

## II

It happened to us babe, even after
the fairground beginning, its many lions.
You were the best straight out of bed.
On top, we'd watch the horizon cut the earth.
Here I knew I loved you, by my doe-ish
need for simplicity: *big, cat, open, yes, please*
*I have to go.* You, completely unharmed by desertion.
Clown. I have been raw as slush for you.
My head, thick on your tongue.
Iced raspberry, illuminated, awaiting our finale
jewelled expectation, for what — rotted
familiar ground, a take two on vulnerability.
At some point, you end up forgiving the conditions —
take what you can get.

## III

Take what you can get & move to Oregon.
You don't have to be blond — just open
to the ways of the axe & wood-fired tubs.
What would my new shape be? I captured
the plane, stuffed it with oil paintings & porn.
The fag's dream is to be pregnant.
Big-dicked homestead, pass me
torched & holy
round a sweet relegation.
Craigslist was provident:
it felt the fattened stack of seasons
waiting to be wanted, the headache
of surrender — fuck my freedom —
the sermons in me — too heavy to attend.

# IV

These sermons in me — too heavy to attend.
But I've got a twenty pack, my sapphire lighter
my nightly staring contest with the statue
over the road. The failure is good, safe
so I practice being hurt. It's impossible
to be alone with a cigarette
or a mirror of stone. Immovable
he too half-believes tomorrow won't come
while minutes tear the seasons into apathy.
My ash & ends pile up. I've already won
against the lovely offer of death.
When fate finally arrives at my mountain
it'll be dressed in burnt punchlines
delivered too late.

# V

Too late to start buying bouquets of stalks.
My friends & therapist say: *keep the beauty for yourself.*
Time blood-runs down the porcelain
as the razor slips on my chin. I lapped
sweat from a star's trebled back.
All cherry-milk, born at dawn
dead by — no — don't let me die —
not without the white want of riven nights
my easy open belly. The girls of Bethnal Green
say *breathe, move girl! onto the next!*
How? There's so much — so much air
I don't know what to do with it
exhaling roll-ups & stems into the contour
of a citizen.

# VI

Being a decent citizen, the doctor asked
*how did this happen?* I'd smoked a flushed cheek
some anonymous man so now I was dying —
faggot as lemming, running off cliffs
after hope in a tracksuit. Nameless
curtains gather the evening, dulled sunrise
putting on clothes — soft traps.
My toenails remind me I'm a weapon.
On the tram to Manchester, I'm chewing
batteries to sharpen my mouth, as I gut
three lads who clocked the queer
the cryptid pulling the cash point out
by its metal lip. Despite all attempts
he's continued to commit the offence of living.

# VII

To commit the offence of living, start with
an idea — which is a sin. I've always been a foal
of stubborn thought, body hot for banishment
for hurling itself on whims like swords.
I've fought, yielded, eroticised ideas
served all my impulse & sucked up solace
from abandoned paintings left by skips.
Fuck it, enough prayer — all our art is hexed.
I can't be wrong anymore. My gold-capped knees
attempt to vanish again — then a sense
of reversal trickling in, the possibility pearlised:
what's done in dark can be done in light.

## On the A56 to Accrington

you took out your cock     reached across the dead
air of your Lexus     unwrapped my fist
& laid it around you.

                    I pictured being found
there in the lay-by like a thief
your stiffness     the evidence

                              the sign
                          cut them clean
                              in two

This is the warm-up     cracked
            & golden
its secret attempting to seal.

Another version of me rolls out the door
            hits the carriageway
soft toy landing on its backside

        fluff still fresh

## Maybe I'll Be A Waitress

Listen. I've decided to go soft. Maybe I'll be a waitress at the bottom of a hot ocean, taking bites out of an apple pie. Or I won't. I'll stuff an office block in my mouth every morning, light the top. I keep imagining impossible things; the way wood hopes it won't grow. I've walked past seventeen crying people & done nothing. Stench of burnt timber at the junction of Frith & Old Compton, currying favour with the clouds. I'd rather be numb than godly — so what — let me commit my offence. Let me slope around this city's body like a coagulant, a cut line. I'll swig cheap beer, enjoy the company of other men. When I'm done, I'll come back to this yew, press my head into the bark so I become a branch. Maybe I'll learn the difference between a return & a retreat, the space between them — a warm stream where I'll bring horses, only to be surprised when they start to drink.

# Hiber

Cut by the bathwater
I study the nature of heat.
How mist moves like a rumor.
I am alone again, steaming time.

*Tell me — what on earth am I going to do?*

My bed becomes another
bed, becomes a fox-den.
Maybe it's the formaldehyde
& not the cigs I love.

What's left but the mind:
a charred plane, shaping frost into thought.
The streetlamp flickers on —
my bones stop gossiping.

There's a verdict stirring.

Best to sleep. Ask such questions
in the dumb morning
when the body is most silent —
the mind growing pink winter.

**wow**

i just wanted to be with everyone…
          my fraud of wasted logic
              gulf of give me a minute
wow! you're reading Siken aloud – WOW!
             & spider legs grow from your chin
       so your face walks away
    into a wet bottle
will you leave me now? never? ok!
       people often sit in green
              desolate places
you can write about this — you can! YES
YOU CAN
my cat, do you want to see her? she's stretched
on my balcony, her sunspot, oh come please! she watches
This Morning & BBC News with me and, and, and
HAH! her day's gone! then the next
she doesn't need this rack after rack
of broken afternoons, it gets so
      unbearable after a while

       do you know what I mean?

## the pearls

after he left     i just kept busy
tied up my concrete guts
recalling the moment he said yes
*at this moment      i could say*
*i love you*              seconds
after first sight      first fuck
then months of build-up
the pearls of potential years
whiter than shock    now
a river of rushing minnows
he wasn't coming back
visitors came instead     left wet ribbons
on my neck    i coloured the concrete with purple
orchids & swollen champagne corks
timeless jokes
of the fucks not fucked
my little monuments
to wishful thinking

## Nude as Retrospect

I'll take it from here. Iron queen,
my shoes are hot with the finale.
Look! The Argentinian place
selling charred green peppers.

It never worried me how big & pale you were.
Months of looming recovery, scabbed
shit brown on the carpet while our mutual
fucks took turns at grinding the time.

One morning, sleepless, we caught a wasp
in the trap of your box-room. Let's steal
the wings, you said, but save
the sting. Ah —

so the violence.
With you, I ate glass & learnt to flicker.
I say I'd fight for love but really, I'd suck any cock
that'd keep me alive.

This is also a fight.
You send the photos, delete the ghosts like I ask.
Is this it? the quietness? the dissolve?
I'm accepting sunlight & requiem.

## fog head

There'll be a last time I have sex
or give my career one more try.
Dogless leash. Consider the prospect
of new meds, light therapy, the venom
of the city. I was born to doom-scroll
thinking age would bring freedom
not calcification. Instead, I salute
every magpie, move my driftwood parts
like a good human should. Wrought
sitting outside restaurants to be told
*Sir, you have to order something to sit here.*
Sentences refuse to prophesize.
I'm smoking again, captured Purpose
with a toothed petal held at its neck
as I thought of Geppetto —
I'll never be a real boy.
The drifting is a vacuum
one final design.

## jean jacket

i bought my body back in denim
a lunchbreak venture
wearing the client
Bond Street caught me
in its boutique windows
i struck a Jimmy Dean
my unprofessional
empty thumbs
monetizing my distant
pockets
the desiring legs
seen through a jewel
of pool water
the price of living
too blue        too gorgeous

## whistle bitch

Slam a door enough times it'll stop whistling. I'm done
with these days of clouded glass. There's an opening
& closing, heat, re-birth, then another, so doped up
on dusk that dogs hang out of me like a van window.
In the gloom, there comes a drum, that my life carries
a drowning, the inevitable ratchet into relapse. Hah!
You can't catch me in here. I'm prepared, my gears all full
of grease. I know by now the wind's a spirit & I'm its bitch.
Or was it the wind all along, twisting me in its pocket?
Whistle bitch.
Huh — here I go again — the stoppered song
I forget so easily.

## There Are No Bombs After 3pm

I met a spy in Valencia.
I asked him what he did
   *auto-motives.*


A muscle of slippers by the front door.
I went back twice, was welcomed three,
all cinema      chilled white Rioja.


He'd no need to teach me
how to hold a blade
at its hilt. I've held
fantasies like sharp objects
all the way down
   all my life.


   *People tell stories.*
   *You tell one, your hands*
   *tell another.*


How long have they danced on triggers
clear as lenses —


He baked me wild mushrooms
while I looked through my glass palms
   a cracked crosshair.

## On Becoming A Mannequin

the air-con sells breath
back to me          ceremonial pleats
surrender to perspex
soft glacier
the dress running over the hardness
hello
my jaw     a billowing collar
my bollocks     a purse of buttons
shopping is an advent
for freezing    into he
she     they     I buy the dress
naked studs unpick the floor's skin
into a lengthening mirror
ah          polarity
bodied by ritual
into crevasse
witnessing collapse
& the joy
of reflection.

## the unfinished business

these days i whittle gratitude
instability slips so easily
like puddles in the roads
we moved from   once   twice
four times before a settling     but kids
are natural nomads   they bounce right back
from jump scares     i wondered why
my mum wore her mother as a party hat
why my dad said if he turned into his father
i should shoot him     one day
they'll move again to homes i can't follow
remember how they worked     haunted
& like all ghost stories I'll blame
the unfinished business   my synonyms for fear
how home isn't a place to rediscover     it's already here or
lost
all the towers i build tumble down   the foundations
wet with effort while i try & learn
to take my human time

# Acknowledgements

I cannot thank Anthony enough — my editor, publisher, & mentor — for nourishing me into the poet I am today. I have grown tremendously under his knowledge, insight, & perception. This pamphlet would have never been written without his teaching. Thank you.

Thank you to Patricia of Out-Spoken for her guidance, hard work, & creativity during my first foray into publishing.

Thank you to Elle, for your priceless friendship, love, & support, as well as your keen professional eye.

Thank you to Shanay, fellow poet & actor, for the good times & reading early iterations of these poems with such grace & care.

Thank you to my parents, for the early encouragement & love of literature, and your unending love & support. I'm blessed.

Thank you to my longtime friends & queer family who have loved & saved me more times than I can imagine — you know who you are.

Many thanks go to The Fenton Arts Trust for the financial support to help create this pamphlet.

Big thank you to the early publishers of my work — *fourteen poems, Impossible Archetype, The Rialto*. Further thanks to the publishers of *The London Magazine* & *Ambit*, where versions of 'Maybe I'll Be A Waitress', & 'On Becoming A Mannequin', appeared respectively.